There Is No Goodbye

There Is No Goodbye

Living With The Loss Of A Child

NANCY KANDAL

FCP

Full Court Press
Englewood Cliffs, New Jersey

First Edition

Copyright © 2013 by Nancy Kandal

Published in the United States of America
by Full Court Press, 601 Palisade Avenue
Englewood Cliffs, NJ 07632
www.fullcourtpressnj.com

ISBN 978-1-938812-18-7
Library of Congress Control No. 2013949331

*Editing and Book Design by Barry Sheinkopf for Bookshapers
(www.bookshapers.com)
Cover Photograph by Karen Bellone*

Colophon by Liz Sedlack

FOR ALL MOTHERS

Author's Note

My son, Joshua Kandal, died by his own hand on the night of December 10, 2010. I slept through that night in blissful ignorance. My husband Rudy and I were awakened at 8 a.m. the next morning by a call that changed our lives forever.

In this third year of grief, I never know when or what will catch me by the heart, doubling me over in pain, tears, and longing for him. Life will never be the same. Yet I function now—able to socialize, exercise, laugh and even be funny.

And I write. I keep writing to live through my pain and to connect with him.

Many of these poems were written in the middle of the night when I couldn't sleep. They were attempts to put into words the depth of my unrelenting grief and sadness, and to allow me the tears, and sometimes the howling, that needed release. The outpouring seemed to help. After a while, it occurred to me that other women going through the same difficult journey might be helped as well.

Thus the publication of my very private feelings. It is my hope that sharing these poems will offer other grieving mothers some additional strength and solace as they cope with their loss.

—N.K.
September 2013

ACKNOWLEDGMENTS

Thank you to Karen Bellone, Dr. Jo Christner, Suzanne De Rusha, Sharon Hagege, Eda Hallinan, Rudy Hornish, Barry Sheinkopf, and Susan Whitmore for their love and support in the writing of this book.

And a thank you to all the friends and family who have stood by me during this time of grief.

I

First dream of Josh
  Not a baby
    A boy
That beautiful curly hair
  Everyone always wanted to touch it
He liked strangers
  Would talk to anyone
Loved Babar books
  I loved them too
My favorite book was the story of the little penguin
  Who couldn't stand the cold
So he went off on his own to find a warm island
  Josh is with him

2

You were floating in my belly
    I was floating on air
You were calm
    I was excited
Then one day after many months those startling eyes
of yours popped open
You decided it was time to start the adventure
You called me mama bear
    And I had your back
You were so damn cute
    No one could resist you
You were healthy and strong
Smart for a little guy
You knew how to be charming
Always ready for adventure
    At eight you were the leader on our safari in Kenya
        No fear
            Just fun
Well there was that one huge black spider in Mombasa
that scared us both half to death
Other than that you were hardly ever frightened of
anything

You wanted adventure
So did I
We were a good team

3

Waking dreams early morning . . .
Finally, you are in my dreams

4

You were so damn cute
Everyone said so
And funny
And strong willed
You were born unafraid
Well, sort of . . .

5

When I think of you or speak of you
A sharp pain runs through my body
And yet I want to talk about you all the time
I don't want to lose you. I never want to lose you.
Love,
Mom

6

Dear Josh . . .
  Dear Josh . . .
    Dear Josh . . .
Yes, all of that and more

7

We chose and agreed upon a name for you
    Joshua
        Your father wanted your middle name to be Terry
        His first name
            Bad luck for Jews
                He isn't Jewish

8

You are in my dreams now
    You appear whole
        The whole Josh as I have known you
Yes, I know you are safe and free
    You certainly are here there and everywhere with me
        Yes, I am your Mama Bear
Is this a test?
    Can I survive without you?
        I'm strong, very strong
I've been tested before
    But this is not a fair test
        Surprise tests are never fair
    Not enough time to study you
        You just disappeared
My pen moves across the paper on its own
    My need to communicate with you so strong
        To hear from you
Talk to me
    I'm your Mama Bear
        Love,
            Mama Bear

9

We could have traded lives
Mine for yours

10

I ache for your pain
    I believe you are safe and free
Still I ache for you

II

There are pictures of you everywhere
Not that I need them to remember you
You are imprinted in my womb
You are the joy and pain of my life
Joy bringing you in
Pain letting you go

12

Rudy holds me tight
I cling to him
Afraid I will fall off the cliff

13

I can't remember the pain of your birth
Only the pain of your death

14

We had fun you and I
We had ourselves some fine fun

15

I have to write so I can go back to sleep
    Getting back into bed is tricky
Climbing over the cat and dog
    Not waking Rudy
Not hurting myself by thinking I'm more agile than I am
    The bedroom is still dark

16

The picture of you at age two
  With that wise flirty look on your face
      Sucking your thumb and holding your blankie
          Sits on my desk
I placed your blankie gently on top of you
  In your banana leaf coffin
      You lying so still
          Looking so peaceful
I was happy to see you again
  You looked so much more yourself
Surrounded by bamboo trees from your garden
  Brought to the memorial by friends and family
How you are so much loved

17

Your absence sneaks up on me
Like a cat on a mouse
I am helpless

18

Anchored by pain
        My back against the sea wall
Waves of grief wash over me
                Yes they scream
                        He's gone
Pushed up against the sea wall
        Waves of grief smash into me
Yes they scream
        He's gone
There's nothing I can do
        He's gone
My knees buckle and I drown

19

It's too much
    Too much to ask
I have landed on my head instead of my feet

20

I don't want him to be dead
Even if I never see him again
I don't want him to be dead

21

You were so loved
     A magnet
Those brown beady eyes
Your love of your friends
     Who love you still
We all mourn for you
     We weren't ready to give you up
     Let you go

22

Waking up this morning from a terrible dream
     Josh is dead
Thank god it was just a dream
      Wait, oh no
          How can this be
Josh is dead
     My heart sinks
         My stomach clinches
     Another day of grief
I take a deep breath
     My chest rises and sinks
        The tears
Another day of grief

23

I wake up wanting to fall back to sleep
    Before I remember
But I do remember
I know
    It will never change
What has happened
    Has happened
No wishing
    No wailing
        No tears
            Or begging
    Will ever bring him back

24

Your pain engulfs me
Strangles me
Tears me to pieces
Where you once lived
I wait for you on a corner in my mind
You never show up in time
The curb is crumbling under my feet
I'm afraid I'll blow away
The sad desperate feeling comes
Without warning or invitation
Takes me down
I know you are not coming back
I don't blame you
I'm just so utterly sorry
You had to leave

25

I scream at you
How dare you take your own life
The life I gave you
Leaving me in this pit of grief

26

Sometimes I get through the day
Like a non-mourning mother
Today I am a victim of my loss
I want your death to be a lie
A bad dream

27

Cleaning up the kitchen
After the beautiful dinner Rudy made
Chicken stir fry
My slow-dripping tears the only seasoning I can taste

28

Waking up to your death
Your forever absence
Living peacefully with your death
Will take the rest of my life

29

I cling to you
  A vine wrapping around the tree of my memories

30

My mind has blown out to sea
    The fog rolled in and I am blind
The rhythm of the waves suffocates me
    I am drowning
This is not a dream
    It's real
I struggle against giving up
    There must be air to breathe
        To float me to shore
When I wake up my mouth and brain are filled with sand
    The me I knew is gone
Thoughts run half way through my head then disappear
    I am adrift in myself

31

The thought of your pain tears through me
  Like a knife
Dropped to my knees by memories
    I feel you have been yanked from my womb
      With the cord still attached

32

I hope my mourning doesn't disturb you
I have to believe that you are at peace now
Or my heart will break and I will die too

33

I will honor your life
        Find a way to honor your life
Make you proud of me
        As I am so proud of you

34

Where are the words
There aren't any
No words
Your pain so strong
You saw no future without it
You will always be inside me
Where you started life
You will never die again

35

Even now to speak of you brings back pain so sharp
And yet I want to talk about you all the time
I don't want to lose you
I never want to lose you
Love,
Mom

36

I wake from a long deep Atavan sleep
You're still gone
All that sleeping for nothing
You are gone

37

I am a prisoner of grief
Let out of my cell for meals and exercise
A little socializing
And then back behind the bars
Pacing and pacing
Wondering if I'll ever get out

38

Sometimes crazy people hear voices
I'd give anything to hear yours

39

I have fallen through the cracks of grief
Been swallowed by pain and mourning

40

I want to go find him
To hold him and comfort him
That is not possible
And even though I am his mother
    There is nothing I can do
        Except let him go so he can find peace

41

So many of us mourn you
We miss you sweetheart
We miss all the wonderful things about you
We understand your struggle and your pain
So now we hold on tight to all the gifts you gave us

42

As a child when I heard someone was "in morning"
It didn't make sense to me
How could a person be "in morning"
Now I understand

43

Dear Josh,

I remember when you were eight and we were visiting Deb in Hawaii. You were constantly in the water on your boogie board. I sat under a tree watching you. Worried but telling myself you were okay.

Every time you got trounced you picked yourself up, carried your board back out into the waves. Yes, I watched with fear and with pride.

You were born brave. No thought of danger. Another time that year you and a friend from school rode your skateboards from 85th Street on the upper east side of Manhattan to the Empire State Building on 34th Street on the West Side. No thought that your mothers might be worried sick that you didn't come home from school on time.

I had no idea where you were. I was worried and angry.

You finally called and said you had just borrowed money from a stranger to call me and tell me you guys were too tired to skate back and that you wanted to take a taxi home and I should wait outside on the curb with money to pay the driver.

Well, I was proud of you. Yes proud. Proud of your independence and the wonderful generous caring man you grew up to be. You were a beautiful human being.

There is nothing else to say.

Love,
Muti

44

I look for you
I still look for you
I want one of those bone crushing hugs
I want to hear you say it
      Mama Bear
Say it

45

There is no escaping
I carry your death with me
Sometimes I forget for awhile
Then when I remember the pain returns
I can't let you go

46

I carried you inside me
       I carried you
I carried you until you walked on your own
I watched you
       I watched you until my eyes closed
No
       I watched you until your eyes closed

47

Now I think of you
Think and think
I hear you so clearly
Oh mom
Oh mom
I hear your pain and it shatters my heart

48

Dear Josh
The stately old oak tree in the yard next door
Has been weeping for you
As I watch the tears fall and the wind blow them
In every direction
I want to run out and catch them
I wish to god and every other deity on earth and in heaven
That I could stop the tears so that sweet old tree would stay green
forever

49

Grief hides at the bottom of the sea
The shark hides behind a large rock
As I swim by it attacks with all its fury

50

More pictures of you
    Of course more
Years and years of pictures
    Stacked neatly and mostly dated
I want them to bring me joy

51

Dear Josh,

Did I ever tell you how proud I am of you? Of the person you turned out to be? Sentimentality made you uncomfortable, so there were lots of times I didn't express my feelings to you. And now you're gone, and I can only hope you knew. In addition to all your people skills and talents, your generosity was incredible.

I am just so sorry you never really got to experience a true love where you let yourself go, where you really let someone in.

Your Mother

52

I want you back
    There's more I have to say to you
        To tell you
    There's more life I want for you
I want you back
    I want one of those big strong hugs that
        Take my breath away

53

Just so you know
I have your Snoopy doll and his sister Belle
And I will keep them safe for you

54

My god
Some of your ashes are within arm's length
You rest in a beautiful wooden box
I need to let you go

55

I miss you
I miss your existence
    Though you are with me every day
I can see you so clearly
        At birth
        As a little boy
        As a young boy
        As a grown boy
        As the man you became

56

What is a mother without her child

57

I am a slave to your absence
In the midst of floating on a wave of laughter
You knock at my heart
And I am flooded by grief

58

Some days are hollow
No need to see anyone
Talk to anyone
Just be Nancy
A quiet Nancy

59

Question:
All the time you spent on beaches
        Did you ever ask a lifeguard for help?

60

As long as I know who I am
    I will celebrate your birthday

61

I hear you saying
  Don't cry Mommy

62

Sometimes
    I don't know why
        I tell strangers you are dead
Sometimes
    I just want to share my grief with strangers

63

Weeping and
Weeping and
Weeping
Will I ever be able to think of you
Without weeping

64

Now wanting to believe in god
   In a hereafter
      That I will see you again
My nipples sting at the memory of your nursing
   Of looking down into that angel face

65

Trying to hold the pain down
It burns in my chest
It doesn't matter where I am
What I'm doing or who I'm with
In the middle of a good time
Friendship, laughter, and love
It just doesn't matter
My thoughts evaporate
And I am in pain

66

Rudy is my Wonder Bread
  With lots of butter and jam
You are my son
  With so much power and strength
    But not enough
And yet I am in love
  Deep exciting and soothing love

67

I am not the only mother who has lost a son
  But I am the only mother who has lost my son
I am not the only mother who has lost a child
  But I am the only mother who has lost my child

68

I am a victim of the bullet that killed my son

69

4:30 a.m.
More bleeding of tears
No bandages
No pain killers
Just pain

70

The first anniversary of your death approaches
I wish you had left me a grandchild
    Flesh of your flesh
        To carry your genes into the future
           To pass on your spirit and goodness
A Baby for me to hold and rock
    As I once held and rocked you

71

No weeping
    No wailing
        No pounding on the walls
No wishing
    Or hoping
        Or dreaming
No anything will ever bring him back

72

This morning I woke with a Josh ache

73

December 10, 2011

The first anniversary of your death
　　We celebrated your life
　　　　Mostly with your male friends
　　　　　　Who have also loved you
　　　　　　Who will always love you and miss you
We scattered some of your ashes on Venice Beach
　　On the volley ball court
　　　　So you would always be there with them
We took your ashes in our hands
　　We held you
　　　　And let you go
I held your ashes sweetheart
　　Held you for the last time
　　　　Then let you blow into the wind
Five of your pals went out into the surf on their boards
　　They released the last of your ashes into the air and waves
The rest of us stood at the water's edge
　　And watched
It was so beautiful

74

I sit with other mothers and weep with them
Sometimes we laugh
Mostly we weep

75

When will I be able to think of you with a smile instead of tears
Will I ever truly understand your choice
Is there anything I could have done to help you

76

I still can't believe it
　　　You took your own life
I wanted to help
　　　Instead I was banished
I am your mother now and forever
　　　Never to have any answers

77

Your birthday again
    Already your second birthday
I want to celebrate your birthdays
    Not mourn your death day
I won't put candles on the cake
    Don't want to count the years without you

78

Three days to your birthday
      I want to celebrate your life
I miss you so much on the one hand
      And feel that you are still with me on the other
And I wonder if this late night weeping will ever cease
I can laugh now, go to movies, spend time with friends

But then it's time to go to sleep
And the knowledge that I will wake in the morning to
      Your mortal absence is just so painful

I want you back
      Even if I can't see you or talk to you
         I want you back alive
Oh honey, it makes me sick to think of you in such pain
      That you would actually kill yourself
You murdered yourself and I feel guilty

Wasn't there something
      Anything I could do to help you
         Comfort you
           Save you

And now I have to save myself
If you were here I would shake you by the shoulders
I would hold you and kiss you
And I would forgive you

79

Me: I'm not angry
Josh: It wasn't your choice to make
Me: True. Everyone makes their own choices
Josh: I was done. I was just done
Me: You were done
Josh: Mom, Muti, Queen of the Wierdos, Mammie,
Mommy,
    Mama Bear, Mother
      I will always be with you
Me: But I can't see you or hear you or hold you
Josh: Yes you can. I'm with you all the time
Me: I want to wake up in your living room where you put
    An extra
        Blanket over me while I was sleeping
  So, Joshie.
     You know I never called you that
     You had the most beautiful curls
     You were the best friend anyone could ever have
When you learned to walk we called you Walkie
When you learned to talk we called you Walkie Talkie
You were so damn cute

80

I would have given my life to save you
I'm not inspired to do anything
Today I'm just stuck in grief
Don't want to talk to anyone
Or see anyone
I don't know whether to put more pictures of you out
    Or put away the ones I have out
I don't know what to do
Everyone has ideas about what I should do
How can I explain
    My son is gone forever
And there is nothing I can do

81

I will never be who I once was
    Whoever that was
I've lost myself
    For a moment I thought I found myself
But this isn't me

82

Wherever I am
Whatever I'm doing
Whoever I with
I am only a shadow of my former self

83

I stare at the ocean waiting for
    What
You to pop out of a wave on your surfboard
I think about Mammoth Mountain waiting for
    What
You to come screaming down off trail on your snowmobile
I dream about your walking in the front door for
    What
One of your bone crushing hugs
I wait for one of the many pictures of you facing me for
    What
You to speak to me

84

You would be forty-two today
My grown up son
The pictures of you taken over the years
From baby to boy
From boy to man
Bring me joy and pain

85

If tears were thoughts
   Then I would be thinking about you all day
Even thinking your name brings on the tears
   And an ache in my belly where you once lived

86

My castle for a cucumber
　　My eyes so swollen from grief
　　　　They hurt to open
Maybe tea bags
　　That might help
It won't take the pain away
Sunglasses for sure so I don't scare anyone

87

Grief is not a race
There is no finish line
No goal
No home run

88

Yes I feel sorry for myself

89

Dear Josh,

There is so much more time I thought we would have together. So much that I never said to you or told you about. So much I wanted for you and me and us. I look at the picture of you and me on my desk probably from fifteen years ago. You have your arm around me and we are both smiling. Me with an open mouth, you with a closed mouth.

And the picture of me standing sideways my face turned away, so pregnant with you. Some of the happiest days of my life.

And the picture of you and me on a camel in front of the big pyramid in Cairo when you were eight.

Thank god for pictures.

I love you sweetheart.

Mama Bear

90

Drowning in sorrow
   Wondering what it would feel like to rise to the surface
      My lungs filling with air and the desire to go on
         With my life
I am not suicidal
   Just so sad

91

The pain you were in has become my pain

92

You were going to live by the sea
Now you will live there forever
    Safe in the sand
        Safe in the waves and wind
That's all I wanted to do
    Keep you safe

93

Oh Josh,
    I know you don't want me to weep for you
        I have no choice
The tears spill down my face
    My nose runs
        I try not to make a sound
I want to howl like the coyotes across the canyon
You would have been forty-three today
    You are an angel now
        No age

94

Yes, you are still your mommy's angel

95

Looking out at the ocean I'm thinking
     If I were a mama whale and you were my baby
     Someday you would swim away on your own

A Message from Josh

"I see you, Mama Bear.
I'm safe, I'm free.
You watched over me.
Now it's my turn to keep an eye on you.
I'll be seeing you, Mama Bear"

ABOUT THE AUTHOR

Nancy Kandal resides in Pacific Palisades,
California, with her husband, Rudy Hornish,
their dog Pookie and cat Litu.

www.ingramcontent.com/pod-product-compliance
Lightning Source LLC
Chambersburg PA
CBHW021934040426
42448CB00008B/1057